science@work
*sports*

# BOOMERANGS, BLADES, AND BASKETBALLS

By Jayne Creighton

RSVP ®

## RAINTREE
## STECK-VAUGHN
P U B L I S H E R S
A Steck-Vaughn Company

*Austin, Texas*

www.steck-vaughn.com

Published by Raintree Steck-Vaughn, an imprint of Steck-Vaughn Company

**Library of Congress Cataloging-in-Publication Data**

Creighton, Jayne.
    Boomerangs, blades, and basketballs: the science of sports /
by Jayne Creighton.
        p.    cm. — (Science [at] work)
In ser. statement "[at]" appears as the at symbol.
Includes bibliographical references and index.
    Summary: Discusses various aspects of sports and
the principles of physics that are involved.
    ISBN 0-7398-0132-5
    1. Physics—Juvenile literature. 2. Sports—Juvenile literature. 3. Force
and energy—Juvenile literature. [1. Physics. 2. Force and energy. 3. Sports.]
I. Title. II. Series: Science [at] work (Austin, Tex.)
QC25.C74         1999
530—dc21                                        99-12288
                                                   CIP


Printed and bound in Canada
1 2 3 4 5 6 7 8 9 0        03 02 01 00 99

**Project Coordinator**
Ann Sullivan
**Content Validator**
Lois Edwards
**Design**
Warren Clark
**Copy Editors**
Rennay Craats
Leslie Strudwick
**Layout and Illustration**
Chantelle Sales

**Photograph Credits**
Every reasonable effort has been made to trace ownership and to obtain permission to reprint copyright material. The publishers would be pleased to have any errors or omissions brought to their attention so that they may be corrected in subsequent printings.

**Ted Bailey**: cover top left; **Basketball Canada**: page 24 top; **Corel Corporation**: pages 4 bottom, 6 bottom, 7, 8, 10 bottom, 14 bottom, 15, 16, 17, 19, 20, 22 bottom, 25, 27, 29 middle, right, 30 bottom, 40, 42, 43 right; **CP Picture Archive (Fred Chartrand)**: page 34; **Eyewire Incorporated**: cover background, bottom, page 30 top; **Sherri Kwasnicki**: page 39; **Mark and Shelley Hepburn**: page 18; **The Naismith Foundation**: page 24 bottom; **R&G Photo (Roy McLean)**: pages 4 top, middle, 26, 43 left; **Sport Medicine Council of British Columbia**: pages 35, 37; **Sweep! magazine**: page 10 top; **Tom Stack and Associates**: pages 11, 32 (Tom Stack), 6 top, 29 left, 38 (Greg Vaughn), 9 (Spencer Swanger), 12 (Bill Everitt), 14 top (Eric Sanford), 22 top (Tom and Therisa Stack), 23, 31, 41 (Brian Parker); **University of Calgary Archives**: pages 21, 33, 36.

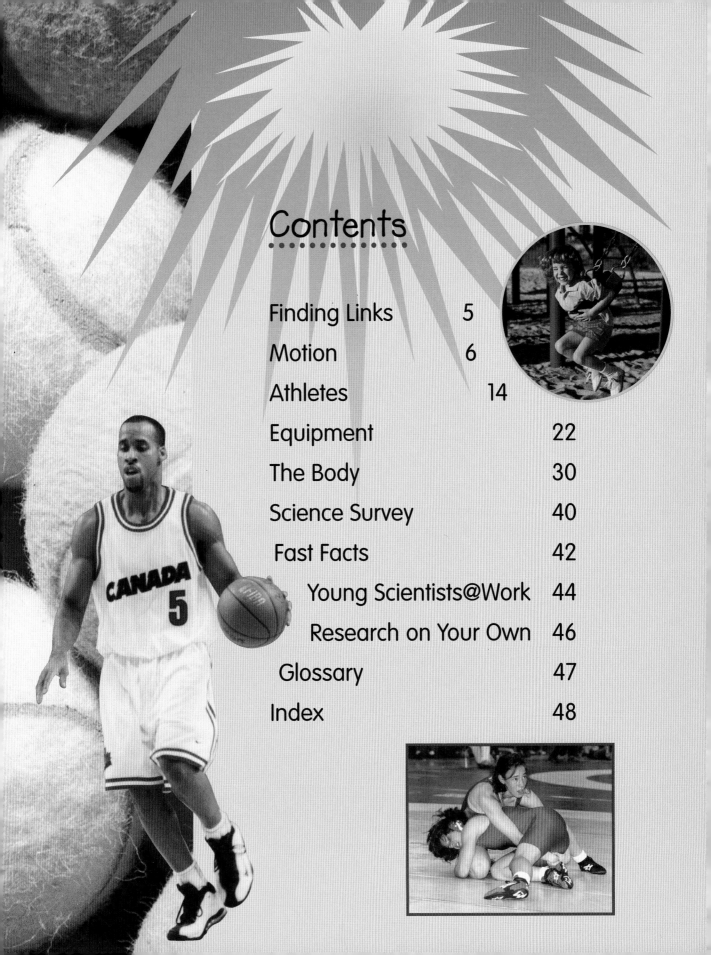

# Contents

# Have you ever

## shot a puck across the ice,

### thrown a baseball,

### or skied along a mountain trail?

You have used the laws of science to make these things happen. Science is all around us when we participate in sports. When you ride a bike or play basketball, you use the laws of physics. When you flex your biceps, biology is involved. When you work out and get thirsty, chemical changes in your body tell you that you need water. Being a good athlete takes more than talent. It also takes science.

# FINDING LINKS

## Society

In the last century, sports have become an important part of society. More people than ever are choosing sports as a career. Because we have more leisure time today than at any other time in history, we can devote more time to either participate in, or watch our favorite sports.

Although sports exist for our health and our entertainment, they can sometimes have a negative effect on the environment. Some motorized sports that use fuel may release exhaust into the air or water. Large areas of land may be cleared to make room for sports stadiums or ski slopes.

## Technology

Technology has made significant contributions to sports. Scientists and engineers are constantly refining sports equipment to help people improve their athletic performance. Developments in **sports medicine** help injured athletes recover faster.

## Careers

Many people are interested in athletics as a career. You don't have to be an athlete to work in sports. There are sports-related jobs in science, medicine, engineering, and teaching.

# Motion

**"Let's get moving!"**

**A**ll sports involve movement. Athletes use their skills to move their bodies and equipment in certain ways. Depending on the sport they play, they may need good balance, good aim, speed, or strength to excel. With a combination of practice and concentration, athletes can achieve the motion they need to succeed.

# How do muscles affect running?

**M**uscles are made of many tiny cells called fibers. There are two different kinds of fibers that make up the muscles that are attached to bones. They are called slow-twitch and fast-twitch fibers. Slow-twitch fibers are dark in color and are used for endurance sports such as long distance running, cycling, or gymnastics. They have a rich blood supply and a good ability to produce energy. Fast-twitch fibers are pale and are able to **contract** very quickly. They are used when the body needs to move quickly, such as when playing football or sprinting. Fast-twitch fibers tire easily.

People are born with different proportions of slow-twitch and fast-twitch muscle fibers. Scientists have taken samples of muscle tissue from different athletes. They have found that sprinters' leg muscles consist of about 65 percent fast-twitch fibers. Long-distance runners' muscles consist of about 75 percent slow-twitch fibers. These differences partly explain why sprinters can run fast for short distances only, and marathon runners can run slowly for long distances.

Muscle fibers are not the only reason for differences in speed. Strength, natural ability, and endurance also play a part. Strength and endurance can be improved with training, but we cannot change the kinds of muscle fiber in our bodies.

| Athlete | Highest Speed |
|---|---|
| Sprinter | 27 mph (43.5 kph) |
| Downhill Skier | 60 mph (100 kph) |
| Cyclist | 50 mph (80 kph) |
| Speed Skater | 30 mph (50 kph) |
| Roller Skater | 27 mph (43.5 kph) |

**BYTE-SIZED FACT**

Triathlons are becoming very popular all over the world. A triathlon includes swimming, cycling, and running. The Ironman triathlon is held every year in Hawaii. Athletes swim 2.4 miles (3.8 km), cycle 112 miles (179 km), and then run a marathon, which is 26.2 miles (42 km).

# How does science help swimmers?

**E**ven though water is not a solid, it provides resistance to movement. Swimmers must use force to push water out of the way. As they swim, another force, called **drag**, is produced. Drag is the force that occurs when a fluid such as water slides over a surface and seems to pull on the surface. Drag always works against the motion of the swimmer in water. As the sport of swimming has developed, swimmers have used their knowledge of science to reduce drag. Improving swimming techniques has been the most important tool for reducing drag. Changes to swimwear have also helped. For example, wearing swim caps and smooth, tight swimsuits allows water to flow over the body more easily.

If you have ever gone swimming in the ocean, you know how different it is from swimming in a lake or a pool. It is much easier to float in saltwater. It is almost as if something helps you float. Ocean water contains dissolved salt, which increases the water's **density**. Density is the amount of a substance in a certain volume. Ocean water is denser than freshwater. Because ocean water is denser, it gives more support to floating objects.

Dissolved salt makes the ocean easier to float in than freshwater.

Good technique and streamlined swimwear help swimmers reduce drag in the pool.

# Why does my bike stay up when I'm pedaling?

You probably remember when you first learned to ride a bicycle without training wheels. It took time to learn to keep your balance. Once you mastered balance, you were able to pedal faster and stay on your bike more easily.

The wheels of a bicycle are two **gyroscopes**. A gyroscope is a spinning wheel mounted on a frame. When the wheel of a gyroscope is spinning, it resists any change in direction. Similarly, when the wheels of a bike are spinning, they help the bike to stay upright. In fact, the faster the bicycle goes, the easier it is to maintain balance.

**Cyclists lean into a curve to turn their bikes at high speed.**

**BYTE-SIZED FACT**

Mountain bike riders use many interesting words to describe their sport and its athletes. For example, a badly bent wheel is called a "potato chip" because of its wavy edge.

# Why is ice so slippery?

**S**kating, skiing, and sledding are all water sports. When you skate on ice, sled down a hill, or ski through the woods, you are really moving over a very thin layer of water. Skates, skis, and sleds put pressure on ice and snow. This pressure melts a small amount of the ice or snow into water. The layer of water allows the skater or skier to glide along the surface. It is more difficult to skate or ski on very cold days because pressure from a skate blade cannot melt the ice as easily as it can on milder days.

**Friction** between sports equipment and snow or ice also helps players in another winter sport. Curling players sweep with a special broom to melt the ice a little and help slide the curling rock into position.

**Curling players use a broom to help melt the ice and guide the rock.**

**Skaters glide along a frozen canal on a thin layer of water.**

**BYTE-SIZED FACT**

There are several different terms for ice of different temperatures. Hockey players like "fast ice," at a temperature of about 16°F (–9°C). Figure skaters like "slow ice," which is about 22°F (–5.5°C). Slow ice is a little softer for landing after jumps.

# Why are ice skaters not dizzy after spinning?

Ice skaters do get dizzy. We all get dizzy when we spin. When people spin, their eyes tell the brain one thing, and their sense of balance tells the brain another.

Balance is sensed by three tiny canals deep inside the ear. These canals are curled in loops and are filled with fluid. When the head or body starts moving or stops moving, the fluid pushes on tiny hairlike sensors in the canals. These sensors send a message to the brain, telling it what the body is doing.

When a person spins quickly and then stops, it takes time for the fluid in the ear to stop moving, just as water in a spinning cup continues to move for a few seconds after the cup has stopped. People feel dizzy because the brain is still receiving signals that say the body is spinning.

When ice skaters stop spinning, they focus very quickly on a stationary object. They also learn to concentrate very hard while their brain sorts out some mixed messages. Doing these things helps them control their dizziness.

Ice skaters learn to sort out the mixed messages their brain receives to control their dizziness.

**BYTE-SIZED FACT**

The oldest known pair of skates is 2,000 years old. Historians have found writing in Old Norse (the old Norwegian language) that describes bone runners tied to feet with thongs. These runners were probably made from the ribs of reindeer.

## What Is Air Resistance?

Air exerts a force that can slow down fast-moving objects. This force is called air resistance. In some sports, air resistance hinders performance.

In a racing sport like downhill skiing, air resistance is a major obstacle. To reduce the effects of air resistance while speeding down a hill, skiers crouch into a rounded "egg" position. They also wear smooth, tight-fitting clothing that allows the air to glide over them.

Bicycle racing is another sport in which air resistance is a problem. Cyclists have special wheels, handlebars, and helmets that are designed to let air flow smoothly over and around them.

New developments in cycling equipment help to reduce air resistance and allow cyclists to go faster.

**BYTE-SIZED FACT**

In 1968 the Olympic Games were held in Mexico City, which is more than 1 mile (1.6 km) above sea level. At such a high **altitude**, the air is thin and there is less air resistance. Because of this, runners ran a little more than 2 percent faster than they did at sea level. Many world records were set at those Olympic Games in the running events, the pole vault, the long jump, and the triple jump.

# How does a pitcher outsmart a batter?

**A** good baseball pitcher knows how to put different spins on a ball to make the batter strike out. He or she knows how to throw a ball so that it curves in an unpredictable direction.

Aerodynamics is the science of the movement of objects through the air. A ball spinning through the air is affected by the laws of aerodynamics. These laws determine the way a ball will move through the air, how far it will go, and how fast it will travel.

As a ball spins, it is surrounded by a layer of air. The stitches on a baseball, the dimples on a golf ball, and the fuzz on a tennis ball help to grab hold of this layer of air. The way an athlete throws or hits a ball will determine its spin. That spin is also affected by different movements of air acting on the ball.

Have you ever been on a moving boat and noticed how the water churns up in a "V" shape behind the boat? This is called a wake. The same thing happens when a ball moves through the air, only the wake behind a baseball is invisible. The chart on this page outlines how different spins produce different wakes that affect the direction of the ball.

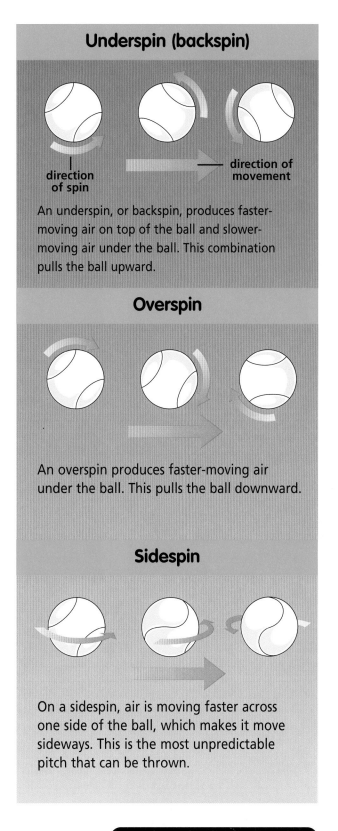

**Underspin (backspin)**

direction of spin — direction of movement

An underspin, or backspin, produces faster-moving air on top of the ball and slower-moving air under the ball. This combination pulls the ball upward.

**Overspin**

An overspin produces faster-moving air under the ball. This pulls the ball downward.

**Sidespin**

On a sidespin, air is moving faster across one side of the ball, which makes it move sideways. This is the most unpredictable pitch that can be thrown.

# Athletes

## "Get out there and play hard!"

**A**ny time you exercise or play a sport, you are an athlete. Some people spend a great deal of time becoming very good at sports. These are the people we usually consider to be athletes. Fitness and skill are important to athletes, who work hard to improve in these areas. They train by practicing their sport, as well as by lifting weights and running.

# LINK TO

## Early Athletes

**People's lives have changed a great deal since the days of ancient Greece, when people gathered in arenas to watch athletes compete. Many of the sports played by the Greeks originated in earlier times, when people's lives depended on whether they were strong and healthy enough to run and hunt.**

Fast runners could escape from enemies. Spear throwers could kill wild animals for food. Strong people could travel farther on foot. In addition, many sports, such as archery, fencing, martial arts, and boxing, have their origins in warfare.

Today, many people still compete in these sports, but their reasons for doing so have changed. People enjoy sports as recreation and as a way of keeping healthy. Some people even earn money by competing professionally.

**Karate originated as a method of self-defense in Japan more than 1,000 years ago. It is now practiced by people around the world.**

**BYTE-SIZED FACT**

Many of the sports that people enjoy today are rooted in games and religious ceremonies that were developed hundreds, even thousands of years ago. The Mayans and the Aztecs both played a court game called *tlachtli* that was a mix of basketball and soccer. The "basket" was a vertical stone ring set 24 feet (7 m) high on a stone wall. Players could use only their elbows, hips, and knees to move the ball into the hoop.

# How do animals play a role in sports?

People are not the only athletes. Since before chariots first circled arenas in ancient Rome, humans have used animals in sports. In ancient Greece, Pakistan, and Africa, the sport of bull vaulting was popular. Cave paintings show that acrobats would catch a running bull by the horns and jump over it from the front to the back. Archaeologists believe either small athletes or children participated in the sport.

Large animals like horses and bulls are still popular in sports. In North America, rodeos draw thousands of people each year. Cowboys test their skills at bronc riding, bareback bronc riding, bull riding, steer wrestling, and calf roping. Horses are used in sports such as show jumping and polo.

In history and throughout the world, people have used animals in races. In ancient Egypt, dogs were used to chase wild animals. In South Africa, there are ostrich races. In Egypt and northeast Africa, camels race against one another.

**Homing pigeons** can be trained to return to their homes when released from a distant place. When the modern Olympic Games started in 1896, homing pigeons were used to carry messages of the event results back to the home countries. Today pigeon racing is a popular sport.

Dogsled races are held every year in Alaska. Participants race teams of dogs over 1,165 miles (1,875 km) of ice and snow. The dogs often wear boots to protect their paws from ice.

**Rodeo events like barrel racing test the skills of both horse and rider.**

**BYTE-SIZED FACT**
The Iditarod is a famous dogsled race. Competitors travel 1,049 miles (1,678 km) from Anchorage, Alaska, to Nome, Alaska, in winter. The fastest time for completing the race is 9 days, 5 hours.

# LINK TO

## The Environment

## Extreme Sports

**Many athletes enjoy sports that allow them to be close to the environment. Some athletes even like the challenge of competing with elements in the environment. They find the challenges they are looking for by participating in "extreme" sports.**

Extreme sports include rock climbing, snowboarding, skydiving, mountain biking, and adventure racing. Athletes use special equipment to reach heights and speeds that might seem dangerous to most of us. They might also venture into wilderness areas with rough terrain.

Rock climbers face the challenge of scaling mountains and cliffs. Snowboarders and back-country skiers, who ski downhill in unpatrolled areas, race on deep snow where avalanches might occur. Skydivers jump from great heights. Mountain bikers ride on rocky ground, up and down hills, for long distances.

The Eco-Challenge is an extreme sporting event in which teams of athletes race across large wilderness areas using rafts, kayaks, mountain bikes, horses, and their feet. Their only guides are a map and compass. Part of the goal of this race is to promote responsible use of the outdoor environment. All competitors in the Eco-Challenge must follow certain rules. For example, racers can only camp and travel where permitted, and they are not allowed to light campfires.

**Rock climbers need strength, skill, and confidence to scale steep rock faces.**

# How can a karate chop break a board?

It is hard to imagine how a karate chop from a human hand can break a wooden board or a block of concrete. When a great deal of force is concentrated on a small area, this is exactly what happens. The action is achieved with a great deal of practice.

First of all, karate masters have thick calluses on their hands. They toughen their hands by pushing them into containers of sand, rice, or gravel.

Karate masters put their whole strength and concentration into the blow. They hit the board quickly and precisely. The hand is held straight out in a "knife" position, with the side of the hand facing downward, or curled into a fist in a "hammer" position.

When seen in slow motion, a board bends before it breaks in two. The upper half of the board squeezes together under the blow, while the lower half stretches apart and starts to crack. The crack spreads upward and breaks the board.

When wooden boards are set up for karate demonstrations, they are supported only at the ends. This gives them more room to bend. Breaking boards with bare hands involves both science and experience. Trying it without experience and practice can be dangerous.

**The force concentrated in a strong blow can split a wooden board.**

## Warming Up, Working Out

**People are learning more about the health benefits of sports. People who are active in sports and exercise keep their heart, lungs, and muscles in better working order. This may help them to live longer.**

Science is helping people to understand how a good diet and exercise improve their health and add enjoyment to their life. Athletes know more now about how to have the best workout without overworking their heart, lungs, and muscles, and causing injury. They understand how important it is to stretch and warm up before exercising and to stretch and cool down after a workout.

Warming up sends blood flowing into the muscles and makes them looser and less likely to tear while playing a sport. Stretching also keeps the muscles, ligaments, and tendons around joints flexible.

A five-minute routine will increase flexibility and decrease soreness. Before running, for example, you can warm up your muscles by walking or jogging slowly for a few minutes.

**Fitness is a way of life for people in many parts of the world.**

**Stretching and warming up keep the body flexible.**

### BYTE-SIZED FACT

The heart is a large muscle. Like other muscles, it becomes stronger with exercise. The heart of a fit person does not have to pump as often as the heart of a person who does not exercise.

# How do surfers stay on their boards?

Just watching surfers riding the waves is fun. It is incredible that they are able to stand up on a small, thin board when it is moving so quickly through the waves. With practice, surfers learn to keep their balance. Balance is important for many sports. In some sports, such as snowboarding, waterskiing, and skateboarding, balance is crucial.

Maintaining balance is connected to a person's center of gravity. Every person and object has one. The center of gravity is the point where an object could be balanced. Most men have a higher center of gravity than women have because they are taller and because they have wider and heavier shoulders.

To demonstrate center of gravity, lay a pencil across an outstretched finger. The place where it balances perfectly is the pencil's center of gravity.

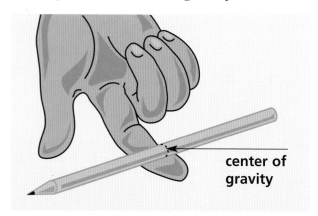

center of gravity

Surfing originated in Hawaii, where it was part of religious ceremonies and prayers. At that time only Hawaiian kings were allowed to surf.

BYTE-SIZED FACT

## Coaching

**If you like sports and enjoy working with people, you may want to become an athletics coach.**

A coach is a person who helps athletes train, practice, and become better at whatever sport they do. He or she may decide what is the best physical training program for a particular sport. A coach also works with an athlete who is practicing, and helps him or her learn how to move in the best way. For team sports, the coach decides which players will play and gives the team strategies that will help them win the game.

A person who used to be an athlete and knows about a sport can become a coach. Some people who wish to become coaches study at college or a university and earn a degree in physical education. A person who simply likes sports and knows about them can become involved in community sports and teams. Coaches work for schools, universities, athletic clubs, and professional and amateur teams.

**Coaches are often former players who have a vast knowledge of the sport they coach.**

Former professional basketball player Larry Bird is one of the greatest players in the history of the NBA. He played for the Boston Celtics for 13 years before retiring in 1992. He now coaches the Indiana Pacers.

**BYTE-SIZED FACT**

# Equipment

**"Can I get new skis this year?"**

**T**echnical improvements in sports equipment have changed the way sports are played. As a result of better equipment, athletes are running faster, climbing higher, and hitting farther than at any time in the history of sports. Every year records in sports are broken. This is due to the combination of better diets, more efficient exercise, and improved equipment.

## Better Equipment Helps Results

**Athletes today are very lucky. They have better pools to swim in, better fields to play on, better shoes to run in, and better bats, clubs, and rackets to hit with than ever before.**

Improved equipment created from human-made materials has greatly affected the results of many sports. This has helped athletes to continually break records.

In the first modern Olympic Games in 1896, the record pole-vaulter reached a height of

| Improvements in Times for the 100-Meter Run | | |
|---|---|---|
| Year | Men | Women |
| 1896 | 12.0 seconds | 12.2 seconds |
| 1936 | 10.3 seconds | 11.5 seconds |
| 1968 | 9.95 seconds | 11.08 seconds |
| 1992 | 9.96 seconds | 10.82 seconds |

10 feet 10 inches (3.3 m) using a wooden pole. In 1940 a man named Cornelius Warmerdan cleared 15 feet (4.5 m) using a bamboo pole. Today, using springy fiberglass poles, athletes are able to clear more than 19 feet (5.7 m).

There have been many other innovations in sports equipment. At the 1996 Olympic Games, rowers pulled newly designed oars with hatchet-shaped blades that move more water. Softball players can hit balls farther with bats made from ultra-light metals. Divers now use boards that provide 15 percent more spring than diving boards that were used in the 1960s.

Pole-vaulters use fiberglass poles to reach greater heights.

# Why do running shoes squeak on the court?

**H**ave you ever noticed when you play on a court or in a gym that when you turn sharply to hit the shuttlecock or move quickly to dribble the basketball, your running shoes squeak?

That is because there is friction between your shoes and the floor. Whenever two objects rub together, they create friction. Friction is the force that tries to stop motion when two objects rub against each other. Basketball players use friction to turn sharply. The soles of running shoes are made of soft rubber that grips the floor, and they squeak from friction when you turn quickly. Friction allows athletes to push against the surface they are on and move forward.

Basketball players would not be able to make quick turns without friction.

**BYTE-SIZED FACT**

Both Canadians and Americans can say that their country was responsible for the origin of basketball. The man who invented the game was a Canadian, Dr. James Naismith. He was a physical education teacher in Massachusetts when he was asked to invent an indoor game for his students. Dr. Naismith came up with the idea of shooting balls through peach baskets.

## Sports Clothing

**The invention of human-made materials for clothing has had a large impact on sports. In addition to being comfortable to wear, these materials may help to improve an athlete's performance.**

Many athletes, such as speed skaters and bobsledders, like to wear spandex, a synthetic material. Spandex is thin, stretchable, and warm. It allows athletes to move faster than ever because it reduces air resistance.

Sometimes natural fabrics work just as well as human-made materials in sports. Many mountain climbers and other winter athletes find that silk provides good insulation from the cold. Silk also offers protection from the Sun. Some athletes wear silk clothes under jackets that are made of a synthetic fiber that blocks the wind and rain, but allows moisture to escape.

**Cross-country ski racers wear spandex to reduce air resistance and increase their speed.**

### Here is your challenge:

**To understand how different kinds of clothing and footwear can affect how fast you run**

**Equipment:**
**pencil, paper, stopwatch, yardstick, or meter ruler**

**Measure 50 yards (46 m). Run the distance 3 times, wearing a different set of clothes each time. Record your times. Compare them, and decide which clothes help to improve your running time.**

1. Heavy coat, boots, pants, T-shirt
2. Street shoes, long-sleeved sweater or sweatshirt, pants
3. Shorts, running shoes, T-shirt

# How do you hit the baseball farther?

**H**ave you ever played baseball and noticed that sometimes you can hit the ball really far? The bat and the ball seem to connect perfectly. The ball soars through the air, and the bat does not vibrate in your hands. You have found the "sweet spot" on your bat.

The sweet spot is the place on the bat that makes the ball go the farthest. There are usually between one and three sweet spots on a bat. When the ball and bat come into contact, **vibrations** travel up and down the length of the bat. At the sweet spot, the vibrations cancel each other out. The lack of vibrations on the sweet spot allows the ball to fly farther when you hit it. Sweet spots are also found on tennis, squash, and racquetball rackets.

To find the sweet spot on a wooden bat, let it hang down and hold it loosely just below the knob on the handle. On an aluminum bat, hold it about one-quarter of the way from the top. Then, tap the bat gently with a baseball along its length, starting at the bottom. As you tap, you should feel a vibration in your fingers. When you hit a sweet spot, you will not feel any vibrations.

sweet spot

**Batters who hit the ball on the bat's sweet spot will send the ball flying farther.**

# How do athletes protect themselves?

The development of safety equipment for all types of sports has saved many people from injuries. Today both professional and amateur athletes wear special clothing and equipment to help protect them from injury. Helmets are worn in many sports. They are made with built-in shock absorbers to protect the head in case of contact with another player or a fall. Safety glasses are worn in many court sports, such as squash and racquetball, to protect the eyes. Elbow pads and kneepads protect joints when people use in-line skates. Life jackets, worn during many water sports, have saved thousands of lives.

Scientists continue to make technical changes to equipment. For example, new rackets are made with shock-absorbing materials. This helps to lessen the impact of repeated hits from a ball. It may also prevent muscle damage.

**Helmets and padding protect goaltenders from fast-flying hockey pucks.**

BYTE-SIZED FACT

Jerry Cheevers, goalie for the Boston Bruins, showed everyone how dangerous it was for a goalie not to wear a face mask. Every time Cheevers was hit with the puck, he put a mark on his mask where the puck hit. Over time, the design of the mask could not be seen beneath all the marks.

# What makes a boomerang come back?

**B**oomerangs were invented by the Australian Aborigines many years ago. They were originally used as weapons for hunting small birds, as well as for sport. There are two kinds of boomerangs. One is a return boomerang, and the other is a non-return boomerang. The non-return boomerang is heavier and larger, measuring 24 to 36 inches (61 to 91 cm). It was developed to hunt large game, such as kangaroos, and to use in war.

The return boomerang is about 12 to 30 inches (30 to 76 cm) long and is shaped in a "V." One side is flat, and the other side is slightly curved, much like the wing of an airplane.

The boomerang is held vertically in the right hand, with the flat part in the palm of the hand. It is thrown forward. The boomerang rises, curves to the left, and glides back to the thrower.

When the boomerang is spinning and moving forward at the same time, the upper wing is going faster than the lower wing. The upper wing experiences a greater **lift** than the lower wing. Lift is the force that pushes an airplane wing upward. The unbalanced lift on the wings of the boomerang causes it to curve around and return to the thrower. Some people have been able to throw a boomerang as far as 300 feet (91 m) before it returned.

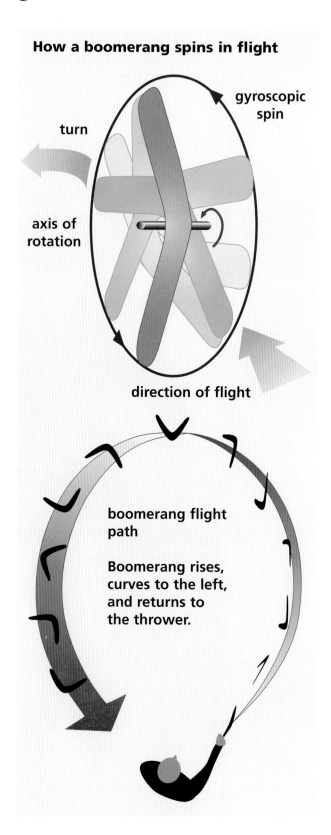

**How a boomerang spins in flight**

gyroscopic spin

turn

axis of rotation

direction of flight

boomerang flight path

Boomerang rises, curves to the left, and returns to the thrower.

# Why do balls bounce?

**A**n object that is being held above the ground has the potential to fall toward Earth. For this reason, it is said to have **potential**, or stored, energy. As the object falls toward the ground, its stored energy changes into **kinetic**, or moving, energy.

When a ball hits the floor, it becomes slightly flattened, and its energy is stored once again. As the ball returns to its original shape, the energy that was stored when it hit the ground changes back into kinetic energy, and it bounces upward.

The amount of energy that can be stored by a ball when it hits the ground depends on what the ball is made of. A rubber ball can store more energy than one made with a less "elastic" material. For example, a rubber tennis ball bounces higher than a leather baseball because it is able to store more potential energy.

Most balls do not bounce back as high as they were dropped. This is because not all of the potential energy changes back into kinetic energy. Some turns into heat energy when the ball touches the floor. Some of the energy also changes into sound energy—that is what you hear when the ball hits the floor.

**The amount a ball will bounce is partly determined by what the ball is made of.**

# The Body

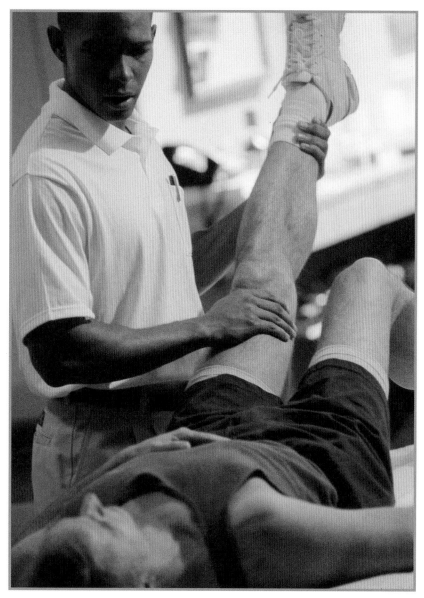

**"I'm glad I warmed up this morning."**

**A**n athlete's body is the most important piece of equipment he or she has. Although exercise is needed to maintain health and fitness, problems can arise if physical activities are not done safely and properly. It is important for an athlete to understand how the body works, and to know how to take care of it. Proper nutrition, injury prevention, and injury treatment are all needed to keep the body working at its best. When all these things are taken care of, an athlete will be able to perform better and have more fun!

# Why is sweating so cool?

Sweating really is cool. Bodies have a built-in **thermostat** at the base of the brain. This thermostat, called the hypothalamus, makes sure everything stays at the same temperature, about 98.6°F (37°C). When people exercise, their muscles produce heat. If the body becomes too hot, it may stop working properly.

During exercise, the body keeps its temperature down by releasing moisture from sweat glands. When people sweat, the moisture is warm, just like the body, and it evaporates into the air. As the sweat evaporates, it removes some of the body's excess heat. Sweating is the best way for a body to cool itself.

**Millions of sweat glands help the body keep cool.**

sweat pore

sweat gland

hair follicle

temperature receptors

blood vessels

Humans have between 2 million and 4 million sweat glands located all over the body. The highest concentration of sweat glands is on the soles of the feet. The lowest concentration is on the back.

**Athletes competing in intense sports need more than sweating to cool their body.**

People who exercise regularly are more efficient at cooling their bodies. This means that athletes sweat faster and a bit more than non-active people.

BYTE-SIZED FACT

## Human Machines

**One area of science looks at sports from a mechanical point of view. This area is called biomechanics. It is the study of how the human body moves. Scientists who test biomechanics think of athletes' bodies as machines.**

Using high-speed cameras and computer programs, these scientists are able to analyze body movements in detail. They can show problems with techniques and how to fix them for better performance.

One test in biomechanics uses a treadmill. Silver dots are attached to an athlete, such as a runner, at points along the body. These dots reflect light onto a high-speed camera. As the athlete runs on the treadmill, the camera takes

**Athletes can test their level of fitness using a treadmill connected to a computer.**

pictures of the moving dots. The pictures are analyzed by a computer. The computer program shows whether the athlete is running in the best way possible, and gives information about what can be done to improve performance.

Even small changes in movement can make a difference in running speed. The test measures length of stride, foot placement, leg speed, and the way in which the athlete lifts his or her knees.

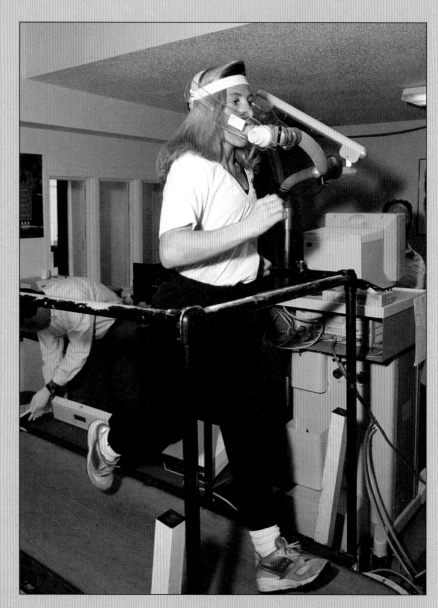

# Why do we breathe harder during exercise?

**M**uscles need oxygen to take energy from food. This energy helps us to move faster. Oxygen comes from the air we breathe and travels throughout the body in our blood. During exercise, muscles use more oxygen than when they are at rest. For working muscles to get enough oxygen, lungs must breathe deeper and faster. When muscles work steadily for long periods of time, they must have a constant supply of oxygen. This type of exercise is called **aerobic** activity.

Muscles can get a little energy from sugar without using oxygen. This energy allows muscles to perform short, intense bursts of activity. When muscles work for very short times without using oxygen,

this is called **anaerobic** activity. However, muscles pay a price for this activity. When oxygen is not available fast enough, a by-product called **lactic acid** builds up in the muscles. Lactic acid causes muscles to become sore.

Sprinting, football, and wrestling are good examples of anaerobic exercises. Long-distance runners and athletes who exercise for long periods of time are doing aerobic exercise.

**During a tough match, wrestlers can build up lactic acid, which causes a sudden achiness in the muscles.**

## Steroids

**Both professional and amateur athletes want to improve their strength and performance in sports. They want to be as strong and as fast as possible. Some people believe that taking drugs will help them become better athletes.**

Some athletes take **anabolic steroids** in the hope of improving their performance. This drug is an artificial type of hormone. Hormones are chemicals that everyone produces naturally in their bodies, but in small amounts.

Anabolic steroids stimulate muscles into taking in more protein, and they help athletes train harder

by helping them recover faster after a workout.

However, there are a number of problems connected with using steroids in sports. Doctors believe the drugs can cause liver damage, high blood pressure, and high cholesterol. Steroids can affect the brain and other parts of the body, and increase the risk of illness. They can also affect moods, making people more aggressive and irritable.

**Canadian runner Ben Johnson won the 100-meter sprint in 9.79 seconds at the 1988 Olympics. Johnson was stripped of his medal when it was discovered that he had been using anabolic steroids, which athletes are not allowed to use at the Olympic Games.**

## Should Athletes Use Drugs to Enhance Their Performance?

The urge to win is very strong among athletes. Some athletes want to take artificial drugs to help them improve their performance. In amateur sports, the International Olympic Committee (IOC) has spent a great deal of time deciding what drugs should and should not be allowed.

The IOC has banned the use of many different kinds of drugs that affect an athlete's performance. Anabolic steroids have been banned since the 1960s. Some drugs are not allowed to be used in some sports, but they are allowed to be used in others. One drug called androstenedione is a type of steroid. It can be legally used by baseball players, but not by football players, basketball players, or Olympic athletes.

The IOC has also banned many drugs that are sold over the counter. Canadian rower Silken Laumann lost her gold medal at the Pan Am Games in 1996. She tested positive for a drug that was in a cold medicine she had taken.

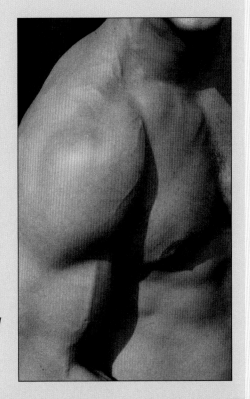

*"If I had known I would be this sick now, I would have tried to make it in football on my own—naturally."* **American football player who died of brain cancer, believed to have been brought on by the use of steroids**

*"I started to see results in about the first week. I felt more powerful and more energetic, able to squat, bench [press], and deadlift more than I ever have before."* **College athlete who took anabolic steroids**

*"I do my weightlifting and take my vitamins. That's it. You have to be careful what you take. It could cause secondary problems with your body."* **Professional baseball player who does not take any steroids**

*"Everything I've done is natural. It's legal and nobody even bothered talking to our trainers. There's absolutely nothing wrong with it."* **Professional baseball player Mark McGwire, who uses the anabolic steroid androstenedione**

**What other points of view might there be about this issue? What is your point of view?**

# Are kids more prone to injury than adults?

Growing children need to be careful when they play sports and exercise. Teenagers are especially vulnerable to injury. Broken bones, strains, sprains, **tendonitis**, and **shin splints** are some of the injuries that happen more frequently in growing children than in adults. They are often caused by overuse of a body part while playing a sport.

Children and teenagers grow very quickly. During growth spurts their bones can grow faster than the muscles that make them move. This makes joints less flexible, so young people have a greater chance of being injured.

Activities that cause the most injuries to young people between the ages of 5 and 14 are bicycle riding, football, games using playground equipment, baseball, and basketball.

**Wearing helmets and proper padding reduces the chance of sustaining injuries in a football game.**

# What is RICE?

Injuries are among the biggest problems for athletes. The areas of the body that become injured most often are knees, shoulders, ankles, and elbows. Sprains, bruises, and pulled muscles are the most common minor sports injuries.

The best way to respond to minor injuries is with RICE—rest, ice, compression, and elevation. Always check with a doctor to assess the injury.

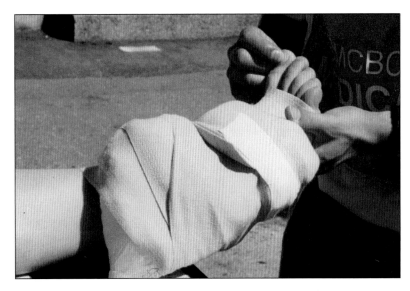

**Wrapping an injury and applying ice to the area can reduce swelling and relieve pain.**

**R**est: Injuries heal faster if the muscles are rested. Using a body part increases blood circulation, which can lead to more swelling in the injured area.

**I**ce: Ice constricts blood vessels and reduces the flow of blood to and in the injured area. This helps to stop swelling and inflammation, dulls pain, and relieves muscle spasms. A one-minute delay in applying ice adds up to an extra hour of healing time required.

**C**ompression: Putting pressure on the injured area by taping or wrapping it in an elastic bandage helps to reduce the swelling. Wrapping an injury squeezes fluids out of the injured site. Skin and tissues cannot expand, so swelling is controlled, and internal bleeding in the area is also limited.

**E**levation: Raising the injured area, such as a sprained ankle, above the level of the heart pulls blood to other parts of the body. Elevation limits blood circulation to the injured area, which decreases internal bleeding and swelling.

# Are sports drinks better than water?

When people sweat, their bodies lose water and **electrolytes**. If people lose too much water, they can become **dehydrated**. Dehydration can lead to fatigue and increase the chances of cramps, heat exhaustion, and heat stroke.

In most cases water is all you need to drink during activities that last for less than 1 hour. For some intense sports that last longer, sports drinks may be better. Sports drinks contain water for rehydration, sugar for energy, and electrolytes to replace those lost in sweat.

Electrolytes are minerals that are very important to the body. Two of the minerals are sodium (salt) and potassium. Sodium helps the body hold onto water. Sodium, calcium, and potassium are all necessary for nerves and muscles to work properly.

Water and sports drinks help to replace the fluids we lose through sweating.

## Make Your Own Sports Drink

**Mix together:**

- 1/4 tsp salt (1 ml)
- 2/3 cup sugar (150 ml) (A package of flavored sugar crystals is a good substitute for some of the sugar. This makes the drink taste better.)
- 7/8 cup (200 ml) orange juice
- 7 1/4 cups (1.8 l) water

**Makes 8 servings**

## Sports Medicine

**Sports medicine is a special branch of medicine that helps athletes stay fit and healthy. The field of sports medicine is growing quickly.**

Many different areas of science and technology are used in sports medicine to help athletes reach their full potential. If you are interested in biology, medicine, sports, and working with people, sports medicine may be a career choice for you.

Doctors, physical therapists, and other health care professionals help prevent and treat sports injuries. Athletic trainers help athletes build physical fitness to improve their athletic skills. Trainers also work with athletic teams and provide first aid to injured players. Sports psychologists help athletes develop good mental attitudes and overcome stress. Sports medicine can help athletes to maximize their workout without causing injuries.

Here are just a few careers in sports medicine:

- Physician
- Exercise physiologist
- Fitness instructor
- Nutritional counselor
- Athletic trainer
- Chiropractor

**Personal trainers offer advice and guidance to help athletes reach goals in their chosen sport.**

**H**ow healthy are you? Do you think you are as fit as you can be? Young people need regular exercise, good food, and lots of sleep in order to stay healthy and grow strong.

# What are your answers?

1. How often do you exercise or play sports?

2. What exercise or sports do you do?

3. How long do you play?

4. What kind of food do you eat each day?

5. How much water do you drink?

6. How much sleep do you get each night?

## Survey Results

What did you find out? Most growing kids need at least 20 to 30 minutes of moderate exercise each day.

Young people need to eat nutritious food every day. The USDA food guide says people need 6 to 11 grain products each day, 2 to 4 servings of fruit, 3 to 5 servings of vegetables, 2 to 3 milk products, and 2 to 3 meat and meat alternatives. Young people need to eat in the middle range of these numbers of servings.

Young people need at least 8 to 10 hours of sleep each night.

## Here is your challenge:

Keep a diary for one week. Each time you play a sport, exercise, or do any physical activity, write down what you do and for how long you do it. Remember, walking or riding your bike is exercise.

Keep a record of what kinds of food you eat, how much, and how often you eat.

Write down how much sleep you get each night.

# Fast Facts

1. Historians have found a stone carving of a skier in a cave in Norway that is 4,000 years old.

2. Olympic wrestler Milo could have been the world's first weightlifter, in the 6th century B.C. One day, he picked up a young calf. He lifted the calf every day until it was fully grown into a bull. The bull weighed about half a ton (450 kg).

3. The first marathon was run by a soldier in 490 B.C. Right after the Battle of Marathon against the Persian army, the soldier ran 26 miles (42 km) from Marathon to Athens to tell about the Greeks' victory.

4. Before football helmets were worn, players let their hair grow long and knotted it across the tops of their heads to form a cushion.

5. Some South Africans play a unique kind of hockey. It is called octopush, and it is hockey played underwater. They play the game with miniature hockey sticks and a hockey puck on the bottom of a swimming pool.

6. Legend says that golf first began in the hills of Scotland when a bored shepherd began hitting small, round stones into nearby rabbit holes with his staff.

7. In 1909 two Olympic medalists set a world record by running a distance of 100 yards (90 m) in 11 seconds. They had their legs tied together in a three-legged race.

**8.** About 80 years ago, baseball players tried playing their game in a swimming pool. Hitters stood in water over their knees, hit the ball, and swam to first base. The base floated because it was made of cork.

**9.** The youngest golfer ever to get a hole in one was only 4 years old.

**10.** The longest tug-of-war in the world took place in 1889. Two teams in India competed for 2 hours and 41 minutes.

**11.** Olympic wheelchair athlete Rick Hansen became a hero when he wheeled around the world to raise money for spinal cord research.

**12.** The youngest swimmer to cross the English Channel was 11-year-old Thomas Gregory of England.

**13.** In 1988 Yves Pol of France set a world record for running 3.1 miles (5 km) backward.

**14.** David Kunst of Waseca, Minnesota, walked around the world. The journey took him 4 years.

**15.** In 1988 a bobsled team from Jamaica competed in the Olympic Games for the first time. The team finished 22nd out of 31 teams.

**16.** The longest race in the world was run in 1929. Competitors ran 3,665 miles (5,864 km) from New York City to Los Angeles.

**17.** The first games of hockey were played by Native North Americans. They played a game called ice shinny on frozen lakes and rivers.

**18.** The stopwatch was invented in the middle of the 19th century. It made accurate readings of athletic and sport records possible.

**19.** In high air contests, some skateboarders have reached heights of 10 feet (3 m) above an 11-foot (3.3-m) ramp. That is 21 feet (6.3 m) in the air.

**20.** Nineteenth century French Canadian Louis Cyr was very strong. He once lifted a platform on his back. On the platform stood 18 men who weighed a total of 4,337 pounds (1,967 kg).

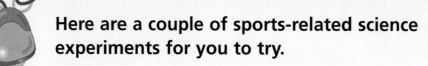

Here are a couple of sports-related science experiments for you to try.

**FACT:** It is easier to pedal a bicycle with fully inflated tires.

**TEST:** Coast, do not pedal, down a hill on your bike, first with your tires fully inflated, and then with some of the air let out of them. Each time, mark the spot on the road where your bike comes to a stop.

**PREDICT:**

Do you think you will go farther on the inflated tires, or on the flat tires?

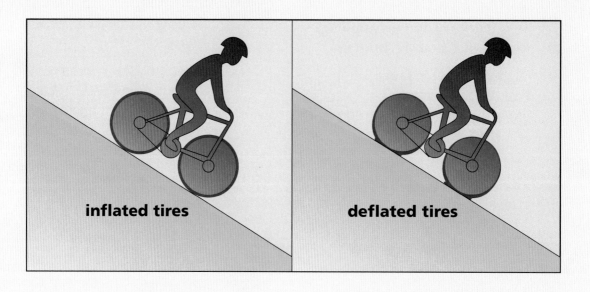

inflated tires    deflated tires

**Answer:** Your bike does not go as far with deflated tires. This is because there is more friction between the tires on your bike and the road. There is more friction when there is more contact between two objects. Your deflated tires have more contact with the road than inflated tires, so it is more difficult for them to roll down the hill.

**FACT:** Saltwater is more dense than freshwater because it contains dissolved salt.

**TEST:** Find two jars, one large, one small. Fill the small jar with 1 cup (250 ml) of tap water. Fill the large jar half full with saltwater. To make saltwater, use 1 cup (250 ml) of warm or hot water from the tap, then mix in 2 T (30 ml) of salt. Stir until all of the salt is dissolved.

Gently place an egg in the freshwater jar. Place another egg in the saltwater jar.

## PREDICT:

What has happened to the two eggs? Why?

Now, remove the egg from the freshwater jar. Pour some of the freshwater into the big saltwater jar, adding it gently down the inside of the jar. Keep adding water slowly. What happens?

**Answer:** The egg in the freshwater should fall to the bottom of the jar. The egg in the saltwater should float. By adding more freshwater to the saltwater, the egg will gradually be suspended in the middle of the water.

# Research on Your Own

There are many places to learn more about sports. Your local library, fitness center, and the Internet all have excellent resources and information for you. Here are some awesome sports resources to try:

## Great Books

**Coulter, George and Shirley.** *Science in Sports*. Florida: Rourke Publications, Inc.,1995.

**Gardner, Robert.** *Science and Sports*. New York: Moffa Press, Inc., 1988.

**Isberg, Emily.** *Peak Performance*. New York: Simon & Schuster Inc., 1989.

**The Ontario Science Centre.** *How Sport Works*. Toronto: Kids Can Press Ltd.,1988.

**Schultz, Ron.** *Looking Inside Sports Dynamics*. Sante Fe: John Muir Publications, 1992.

**Sheely, Robert, and Bourgeois, Louis.** *Sports Lab, How Science Has Changed Sports*. New York: Silver Moon Press, 1994.

## Great Websites

**Educational information from Cislunar Aerospace Inc.**
http://wings.ucdavis.edu/Activities/intermediate.html

**Hillary Sports Organization**
http://www.hillarysport.org.nz/kids/hyper/hyper_8/intern_8.html

**Science of Sports**
http://www.livjm.ac.uk/sports_science/info.htm

**Sports Illustrated for Kids**
http://www.sikids.com/index.html

**Youth Sports Network**
http://www.ysn.com/

# Glossary

**aerobic exercise:** Exercise that requires an adequate and continuous supply of oxygen

**altitude:** Height above sea level

**anabolic steroids:** Artificial substances that act like hormones to promote the growth of muscle tissue

**anaerobic exercise:** Exercise that uses energy obtained without using oxygen

**contract:** To become shorter and thicker

**dehydration:** Unhealthy loss of water from the body

**density:** The amount of a substance in a certain volume

**drag:** The force exerted by gas or liquid on any object moving through it

**electrolytes:** Substances that dissolve in water and conduct electricity. The body uses electrolytes in many of its chemical reactions.

**friction:** The force that opposes motion when two objects rub against each other

**gyroscope:** A wheel that spins on its axis and is able to maintain its original direction

**homing pigeons:** Pigeons that were developed for their ability to return home after traveling great distances

**kinetic energy:** Energy that is associated with a moving body

**lactic acid:** A by-product that builds up in muscles that are working anaerobically. It causes muscle soreness.

**lift:** A force that raises an object against the force of gravity

**potential energy:** Energy that is stored in an object

**shin splints:** Injury of some of the front leg muscles, caused by activities such as running.

**sports medicine:** The science of prevention and treatment of sports injuries

**tendonitis:** Inflammation and swelling of the tendon, the band that connects muscle to bone

**thermostat:** A device that senses temperature and automatically adjusts it if necessary

**vibrations:** Very small, very fast back-and-forth or up-and-down movements

# Index